فضل الإسلام

The Merit of Islām

Title:
The Merit of Islām

Author:
Shaykh Muḥammad bin 'Abdul-Wahhāb
[raḥimahullāh]

Editor: 'Imrān Ḥussain

Taqrīẓ:

Shaykh Naẓīr Aḥmad bin 'Abul-Wāhid

(Bahrain)

Translation edited & checked by:

Abu Khuzaimah al-Ansari

(Salafiri, UK)

Special thanks to: Fazl Khan (UK)

Edition: 1st (only English)

1

Visit: **takhrijalhadith-bookstore.net**

Contact **sales@takhrijalhadith.com**
for wholesale orders.

Follow us on **Social Media:**

Linktree: https://linktr.ee/takhrijalhadith

Contents

Foreword
of the publisher

Indeed, all praise is for Allāh. We praise Him and we seek His help. Whomsoever Allāh guides, there is no one to misguide him, and whoever He leads astray, there is no one to guide him. And I bear witness that none has the right to be worshipped but Allāh, alone, Who has no partner, and that Muḥammad is His slave and His Messenger. To proceed:

Before you is the English rendition of the treatise "Faḍlul-Islām" - "The Merit of Islām" by Shaykh Muḥammad bin 'Abdul-Wahhāb, may Allāh have mercy on him. This concise book contains the distinctive characteristics of Islām, and if someone ponders over each chapter and the proofs mentioned within it, he will be able to recognize many of the great blessings of Islām and its merit over other religions. This book is one that rewards reflection and contemplation, so each chapter should be accompanied by such.

To increase its usefulness to the reader, the authentication of this book by Shaykh Zubayr ʿAlī Za'ī, may Allāh have mercy on him, has been added. In this way, this book can be used both as a companion when listening to a scholarly explanation and for self-study.

The translation has been revised and edited by our noble brother Abu Khuzaimah al-Ansari from Salafi Research Institute (UK); brother Fazl Khan (UK) helped with important organizational matters, may Allāh reward them both with the best of rewards, Ameen.

The Taqrīẓ was written by Shaykh Naẓīr Aḥmad bin 'Abul-Wāhid, who graduated from the famous Jāmi'a Darussalām 'Umrabād (India), holds a bachelor's degree in Ḥadīth and a master's degree in Fiqhul-Ḥadīth from Medīnah University and a PhD from the International Islamic University (Malaysia) on the life and works of Sayyid Nadhīr Ḥusayn Muḥaddīth Dhelwī [raḥimahullāh]. He currently works as an Islamic researcher and advisor to the Bahraini Awqāf, may Allāh protect and preserve him, Ameen.

'Imrān Ḥussain

Takhrīj al-Ḥadīth Publications, 9th May 2022

Taqrīẓ
by Shaykh Naẓīr Aḥmad bin 'Abul-Wāhid

In the name of Allāh the Most Beneficent, the Most Merciful.

All praise is for Allāh, and may blessings and peace be upon the Messenger of Allāh. To proceed:

I was pleased to learn that Brother 'Abdullāh Ṭāriq and his team intend to publish the English translation of the treatise "The Merit of Islām", which was written by the Shaykh, the Imām, the Mujaddid, Muḥammad bin 'Abdul-Wahhāb at-Tamīmī, may Allāh have mercy on him. It is a short and beneficial treatise on the virtues of Islām and the obligation of people to embrace it. It also contains exhortations to follow the Sunnah and warning against innovations. The author also addresses the strangeness of Islām and its followers at the end of times. The mention of the Takhrīj of the Aḥadīth of this book by the Shaykh, the Muḥaddith, Abū Mu'ādh Zubayr 'Alī Za'ī al-Afghānī, al-Pakistānī, who is among the well-known Pakistānī Muḥaddithīn of recent times, may Allāh have mercy on him, has added an additional value to this scholarly treatise.

I ask Allāh, the Mighty and Majestic, that He rewards those who have worked on the publication of this treatise with the best reward, and that He facilitates its access to the greatest number of Muslims and even non-Muslims, so that its benefit may spread, and that it may lead people to return to the religion of Allāh, besides which Allāh accepts no religion. And all praise is due to Allāh, the Rabb of the Worlds, and blessings and peace be upon the Trustworthy Messenger.

Written by the one who hopes for forgiveness from his Rabb,

Nadhīr Aḥmad Ibn 'Abdul-Wāḥid Chaudrī,

Rifā', Kingdom of Baḥrain

Date: 6th Shawwāl 1443 Hijrī / 7th May 2022

Foreword

All praise is for Allāh, Rabb of the Worlds, and peace and blessings be upon the Master of the Messengers, our Prophet Muḥammad, and upon his family and all of his companions. To proceed:

Indeed, Allāh has favoured us with the great religion of Islām, which He has made a complete religion and has thereby completed His favour upon this Ummah, as He says: **"On this day I have perfected your religion, completed My favours to you, and have chosen Islām as your religion..."** [Sūrah Mā'idah 5:3] And Islām is what is referred to in the statement of the Most High: **"Truly, the religion with Allāh is Islām."** [Sūrah Āl-'Imrān 3:19] and it is explained in detail in the "Ḥadīth of Jibrīl" in terms of belief, actions and its branches (see Ṣaḥīḥ al-Bukhārī: 50, Ṣaḥīḥ Muslim: 9).

This book "The Merit of Islām" by the illustrious Imām, Muḥammad bin 'Abdul-Wahhāb, may Allāh have mercy on him, has great importance with regards to understanding Islām and its virtue. Our Ustādh Ḥāfiz Zubayr 'Alī Za'ī [rahimahullāh] has made efforts to authenticate and annotate it. He has graded the Aḥadīth in the book according to the principles of Ḥadīth sciences, may Allāh reward him for the efforts he has made.

I hope from Allāh that every Muslim benefits from this book.

And I ask Allāh, the Great, Rabb of the great Throne, that He forgives our two Shaykhs and pardons them and that He rewards them both and that He gathers us all in the Garden of Abode, for indeed He is able to do that, what an excellent Guardian and an excellent Helper.

Ḥāfiẓ Nadīm Ẓahīr

12th Shaʿbān 1436AH/May 2015

In the name of Allāh, the Most Gracious, the Most Merciful

Foreword to the treatise:
The Merit of Islām

Indeed, all praise is for Allāh. We praise Him and we seek His help. Whomsoever Allāh guides, there is no one to misguide him, and whoever He leads astray, there is no one to guide him. And I bear witness that none has the right to be worshipped but Allāh, alone, Who has no partner, and that Muḥammad is His slave and His Messenger. To proceed: Indeed, the best Speech is the Book of Allāh, and the best guidance is the guidance of Muḥammad [[salallāhu 'alayhi wa sallam]], and worst of affairs are the newly invented matters [in the religion] and every innovation is misguidance.

This is the treatise "The Merit of Islām" by Shaykh al-Mujāhid, al-Mujaddid, Shaykhul-Islām Muḥammad bin 'Abdul-Wahhāb bin Sulaymān at-Tamīmī, may Allāh have mercy on him.

I relied on the printed edition in "Mu`allafāt ash-Shaykh al-Imām Muḥammad bin 'Abdul-Wahhāb"[1] with the corrections of Shaykh Ismā'īl

---

(1) [Editor: Mu`allafāt ash-Shaykh al-Imām Muḥammad bin 'Abdul-Wahhāb [1/203-227] 1st edition. Riyadh: Jam'e al-Imam Muhammad bin Sa'ūd al-Islāmiyyah). To make this bilingual edition easier to use, punctuation, paragraph breaks, and the use of boldface are slightly different to the original.]

[Note: For details on the principles applied by the Shaykh in evaluating Aḥadīth, see his commentary on Ikhtiṣār 'Ulūm

al-Anṣārī, Muḥammad 'Īd, 'Abdul-'Azīz bin Ibrāhīm al-Farīḥ and Ṣāliḥ al-Muḥammad al-Ḥasan.

I referenced the Aḥādīth and Āthār and graded their authenticity or weakness based on my research and I did this while referring to the fundamentals of Ḥadīth and trusted principles according to the Imāms of Ḥadīth, may Allāh increase the light [in their graves]. When faced with conflicting views regarding a narrator, I took the view of the majority [of Ḥadīth scholars]. And there is no success except from Allāh, on Him I rely and to Him I turn back.

Ḥāfiẓ Zubayr 'Alī Za'ī

20th Mai 2013

---

al-Ḥadīth by Imām Ibn Kathīr or his research articles on the subject.]

A Summarised Biography

of Shaykh Muḥammad bin 'Abdul-Wahhāb at-Tamīmī, may Allāh have mercy on him

His name and lineage: Muḥammad bin 'Abdul-Wahhāb bin Sulaymān bin 'Alī bin Muḥammad bin Aḥmad bin Rāshid at-Tamīmī al-'Adnānī, may Allāh have mercy on him.

His Birth: 1115AH [1703CE] in Dir'iyyah.

His Shuyūkh: He took knowledge from many scholars. They include:

1. His father 'Abdul-Wahhāb bin Sulaymān,

2. Shihābud-Dīn al-Mawsali, the Judge of Baṣrah,

3. Ḥasan al-Islāmbūlī,

4. 'Abdullāh bin Muḥammad bin 'Abdul-Laṭīf al-**Aḥ**sā`ī,

5. Zaynud-Dīn Maghribī,

6. Ḥasan at-Tamīmī,

7. Muḥammad Ḥayāt as-Sindhī,

8. Muḥammad al-Majmū'ī,

9. Yūsuf Āl-Sayf,

10. 'Abdullāh bin Ibrāhīm bin Sayf al-Madanī,

and others, may Allāh have mercy upon all of them.

His students: Many scholars took knowledge from him, they include:

1. Aḥmad bin Rāshid al-'Arīnī, the Judge of Sudayr,

2. Ḥamad bin Ḥusayn,

3. Ḥamad bin Ibrāhīm,

4. 'Alī bin Muḥammad bin 'Abdul-Wahhāb,

5. Ḥusayn bin Muḥammad bin 'Abdul-Wahhāb,

6. Ibrāhīm bin Muḥammad bin 'Abdul-Wahhāb,

7. 'Abdullāh bin Muḥammad bin 'Abdul-Wahhāb,

8. Aḥmad bin Nāṣir bin 'Uthmān bin Ma'mar,

9. Aḥmad bin Suwaylim,

10. Ḥusayn bin 'Abdullāh, the Judge of Ḥaramalā`,

and many others were his students, may Allāh have mercy upon all of them, extensive mercy.

The scholars who praised him: Many scholars praised him. They include:

1. 'Allāmah ash-Shām, 'Abdul-Qādir bin Badrān said: "The Atharī 'Ālim, the great scholar Muḥammad bin 'Abdul-Wahhāb..." see the book 'Ulamā` an-Najd Khilāl Thamāniyah Qurūn, [1/142].

2. Al-'Allāmah Muḥammad bin Ismā'īl al-Amīr aṣ-Ṣan'ānī, the author of Subulus-Salām. He wrote a famous poem supporting the Shaykh.

3. Shaykh Muḥammad Bashīr as-Sahsawānī, the author of Ṣiyānatul-Insān 'an waswasatu Daḥlān, defended him and it was a strong defence.

4. Shaykh Muḥammad bin Nāṣir bin Ma'mar, defended him and it was brilliant defence.

5. The sons of the Shaykh, and Shaykh Ḥasan and others.

6. Al-'Allāmah Muḥammad bin 'Alī ash-Shawkānī, who praised his Da'wah efforts and has some amazing lines of poetry praising him.

I say: the Ahlul-Ḥadīth and the people of Tawḥīd unanimously agree on his trustworthiness, in praising him and defending him, and he was a trustworthy Mujāhid, Muwaḥḥid, Mujtahid and a follower of the Qurān and Sunnah, may Allāh have mercy on him.

His works: He has numerous beneficial works. Some of them are:

1. Kitāb at-Tawḥīd al-ladhī huwa ḥaqqullāh 'alal-'Abīd

2. Mukhtaṣar Sīrah an-Nabawiyyah

3. Mukhtaṣar Zād al-Ma'ād

4. Uṣūl al-Īmān

5. Masā`il al-Jāhiliyyah

6. Al-Kabā`ir

7. Kashf ash-Shubuhāt

8. Faḍl al-Islām

His Death: 1206AH.

I say: I summarized this biography from the book "Daḥr Iftira`āt Ahl-az-Zaygh wal-Irtiyāb 'an da'wah al-Imām Muḥammad bin 'Abdul-Wahhāb".

For detailed biographies, refer to:

1. Muḥammad bin 'Abdul-Wahhāb, Muṣliḥ, Maẓlūm, Muftarī 'alayh by Shaykh Mas'ūd 'Ālam an-Nadwī,

2. Muḥammad bin 'Abdul-Wahhāb, Mujaddid al-Qarn ath-Thānī 'Ashr by 'Allāmah Aḥmad bin Ḥajr al-Buṭāmī al-Ban'alī,

3. Min Mashahīr al-Mujaddidīn fil-Islām, by Shaykh Ṣāliḥ bin Fawzān al-Fawzān,

and other beneficial books.

Chapter
The Merit of Islām

Allāh, the Most High, says: **"On this day I have perfected your religion, completed My favours to you, and have chosen Islām as your religion..."** [Sūrah Mā'idah 5:3]

And He says: **"Say: O you mankind! If you are in doubt as to my religion, then [know that] I will never worship those whom you worship, besides Allāh. But I worship Allāh Who causes you to die."** [Sūrah Yūnus 10:104]

And He says: **"O you who believe! Fear Allāh and believe too in His Messenger [Muḥammad [salallāhu 'alayhi wa sallam]], He will give you a double portion of His Mercy, and He will give you a light by which you shall walk [straight], and He will forgive you. And Allāh is Oft-Forgiving, Most Merciful."** [Sūrah al-Ḥadīd 57:28]

And it is reported in aṣ-Ṣaḥīḥ from Ibn 'Umar, may Allāh be pleased with Him and His father: the Messenger of Allāh [salallāhu 'alayhi wa sallam] said: "Your example and the example of the people of the two Scriptures [i.e., Jews and Christians] is like the example of a man who employed some laborers and asked them: "Who will work for me from morning till midday for one Qīrāṭ?" The Jews [accepted and] carried out the work. He then asked: "Who will work for me from midday up to the 'Aṣr prayer for one Qīrāṭ?" The Christians fulfilled the work. He then said: "Who will work for me from the 'Aṣr till sunset for two Qīrāṭ?" You [Muslims] are those people. The Jews and the

Christians got angry and said: "Why should we work more and get less reward?"[2] [Allāh] said: "Have I withheld any part of your right?" They said: "No." He said: "It is My Blessing; I bestow upon whomever I wish."[3]

And also from Abū Hurayrah, may Allāh be pleased with him, he said: The Messenger of Allāh [salallāhu 'alayhi wa sallam] said: "Allāh diverted Friday from those who were before us. For the Jews [the day set aside for prayer] was Saturday, and for the Christians it was Sunday. And Allāh turned towards us and guided us to Friday [as the day of prayer]. In fact, He [Allāh] made Friday, Saturday, and Sunday [as days of prayer] and in this order would they [Jews and Christians] come after us on the Day of Resurrection."[4] And it has been mentioned Ta'līqan [in annotative form] from the Messenger of Allāh [salallāhu 'alayhi wa

---

Everything between two square brackets [ ] has been added by the researcher i.e. Shaykh Zubayr 'Alī Za`ī [raḥimahullāh] or the editor, which is marked [Editor...].

[2] In another manuscript of Ṣaḥīḥ al-Bukhārī: "...and we get less?", and the meaning is the same.

[3] Ṣaḥīḥ al-Bukhārī [2268].

[4] Ṣaḥīḥ Muslim [22/856] and it is his wording. There is another chain of transmission for this Ḥadīth in Ṣaḥīḥ al-Bukhārī [876] and others. [Editor: The first number in the reference for Ṣaḥīḥ Muslim refers to the Ḥadīth number in the relevant book, so in this case Ḥadīth [22] in Kitāb al-Jumu'ah and Ḥadīth [856] in Ṣaḥīḥ Muslim without counting the repetitions].

sallam]: "The most beloved religion to Allāh is the simple Ḥanifiyyah." [5]

And from 'Ubayy bin Ka'b, may Allāh be pleased with him, he said: "Upon you is the straight path and the Sunnah. Whoever follows the straight path and the Sunnah and remembers Allāh and his eyes fill with tears from fear of Allāh, then the Fire will not touch him. And whoever follows the straight path and the Sunnah and remembers Allāh and has goose bumps from the fear of Allāh, he will be like a tree that has withered leaves, and his sins will fall off from him as the leaves fall off from that tree. And being moderate on the Sunnah is better than striving in what opposes the straight path and the Sunnah." [6]

And from Abū Dardā`, may Allāh be pleased with him, he said: "O wonder! How good is the sleeping, eating, and drinking of the wise! How do they surpass those being awake [at night] and the fasting of fools? Righteousness, together with

---

(5) Ṣaḥīḥ al-Bukhārī [before Ḥadīth 39] Ta'līqan. [Editor: Here Ḥanifiyyah means: "Islāmic Monotheism i.e., to believe in the Oneness of Allāh and to worship Him [Allāh] Alone and not to worship anything else along with Him.", see Ṣaḥīḥ al-Bukhārī [1/74] in the English Translation by Dr. Muḥsin Khān].

(6) **Ḥasan:** Transmitted by Imām Aḥmad in az-Zuhd [pp. 137-138, Ḥadīth 737], and Abū Nu'aym in Ḥilyatul Awliyā` [1/253] with a slight variation and a chain that is Ḥasan li-dhātihi [i.e. good by itself].

Taqwā and firm faith is heavier, greater, superior, and better than the worship of the heedless."[7]

Chapter

The obligation of [embracing] Islām

Allāh, the Most High, says: **"Anyone who seeks a religion other than Islām, never will it be accepted from him; and in the Hereafter he will be among the losers."** [Sūrah Āl-'Imrān 3:85]

And He says: **"Truly, the religion with Allāh is Islām."** [Sūrah Āl-'Imrān 3:19]

And He says: **"This is My straight path; follow it and do not follow other ways, lest they lead you away from His way. This is what He commands you, so that you may become righteous."** [Sūrah al-An'ām 6:153] Mujāhid said: "The word 'other ways' refers to the [religious] innovations and misconceptions."[8]

'Ā`ishah, may Allāh be pleased with her, narrates, the Messenger of Allāh [salallāhu 'alayhi wa sallam] said: "Anyone who innovates something in this matter of ours [Islām] that is not part of it, will have it rejected."[9] In another wording: "Whoever does any action that is not a part of this affair of ours [Islām] will have it rejected."[10]

---

(8) **Sanad Ḍa'īf**: Ibn Jarīr aṭ-Ṭabarī narrates this in his Tafsīr [8/88] from the route of 'Abdullāh bin Abī Nujayḥ from Mujāhid. It is also narrated in the Tafsīr attributed to Imām Mujāhid [1/227]. 'Abdullāh bin Abī Nujayḥ is a Mudallis and narrated with "عن" here, and it is said he took this from Qāsim bin Abī Bazzah [who is Thiqah], and Allāh knows best.

(9) Ṣaḥīḥ al-Bukhārī [2697] and Ṣaḥīḥ Muslim [17/1718].

(10) Ṣaḥīḥ Muslim [18/1718] and in al-Bukhārī Ta'līq form [before Ḥadīth 7350-7351].

And it is narrated in al-Bukhārī from Abū Hurayrah, may Allah be pleased with him, he said: The Messenger of Allāh [salallāhu 'alayhi wa sallam] said: "All of my Ummah will enter Paradise except those who refuse." It was said: 'Who would refuse, O Messenger of Allāh?' He said: "He who obeys me shall enter Paradise, and he who disobeys me has indeed refused."[11]

And it is narrated in aṣ-Ṣaḥīḥ that Ibn 'Abbās, may Allah be pleased with him and his father, the Messenger of Allāh [salallāhu 'alayhi wa sallam] said:

"The most hateful people to Allāh are three: An evildoer in the Ḥaram [the Islamic sanctuaries in Makkah and Madinah]; he who innovates something into Islām from the aspects of Jāhiliyyah [pre-Islāmic period of ignorance]; and he who seeks to shed somebody's (a Muslims) blood without any right." Narrated by al-Bukhārī.[12]

(Ibn Taymiyyah said regarding his statement "something from the aspects of Jāhiliyyah":) It is applicable to any general or specific conduct of certain individuals; be it part of the religion of the People of the Book [Jews and Christians],

---

(11) Ṣaḥīḥ al-Bukhārī [7280].

(12) Ṣaḥīḥ al-Bukhārī [6882]. [Editor: The wording in the book by Shaykh Muḥammad bin 'Abdul-Wahhāb, may Allāh have mercy on him, has: "He who seeks to shed the blood of a Muslim..." The word "Muslim" is not present in the printed editions that are available].

Paganism, or anything else contradicting what the messengers came with.(13)

And it is narrated in aṣ-Ṣaḥīḥ from Ḥudhayfah, may Allāh be pleased with him, he said: "Follow the straight path, O community of reciters, for then you have taken a great lead. And if you deviate to the right or left, you will go far astray."(14)

And it is narrated from Muḥammad bin Waḍḍāḥ, he would enter the Masjid and stand at the circles [of learning] and he said [as is mentioned in the narration before].(15) He once said: "Ibn 'Uyaynah related to us from Mujālid from Sha'bī from Masrūq that 'Abdullāh bin Mas'ūd said: "There is no year, except that it is certainly followed by a worse one. I do not mean that a year is more prosperous than another, nor that a leader is better than another. Rather, I am referring to the passing away of your scholars and the best of you. Then, a people will emerge who evaluate

---

(13) [Editor: see Iqtiḍā' aṣ-Ṣirāṭ al-Mustaqīm li Ibn Taymiyyah, 1/259].

(14) Ṣaḥīḥ al-Bukhārī [7282].

(15) **Sanad Ḍa'īf**: See the book "Al-Bida'u wa-nahī 'anhā" by Muḥammad bin Waḍḍāḥ [17, and in another edition with the Taḥqīq of Badr bin 'Abdullāh al-Badr: 13] and as-Sunnah li Marwazī [57].

It has defects, and from them is that al-A'mash is a Mudallis and he narrates with "عن", and the previous narration is sufficient in this regard.

affairs/matters based on their opinions, and so Islām will be ruined and harmed."[16]

(16) **Sanad Ḍa'īf**: Al-Bida'u wa-nahī 'anhā [81, and in another edition: 78], Sunan ad-Dārimī [1/76, Ḥadīth 188]. Mujālid bin Sa'īd is weak, the majority of scholars declared him to be weak, refer to Majma' az-Zawā`id [9/416].

Chapter
The meaning of Islām

Allāh, the Most High, says: **"Then if they argue with you, say, "I have submitted myself to Allāh, and so have those who follow me.""** [Sūrah Āl-'Imrān 3:20]

And it is narrated in aṣ-Ṣaḥīḥ from 'Umar bin al-Khaṭṭāb, may Allāh be pleased with him, the Messenger of Allāh [salallāhu 'alayhi wa sallam] said: "Islām is to testify that none has the right to be worshipped but Allāh and that Muḥammad is the Messenger of Allāh, to establish the prayer, pay the Zakāh, fast the month of Ramaḍān, and perform Ḥajj of the Sacred House if you have the means for it."[17]

And in this regard, it is narrated from Abū Hurayrah, may Allāh be pleased with him, in Marfū' form [i.e., from the Prophet [salallāhu 'alayhi wa sallam]]: "A Muslim is the one from whose tongue and hand the Muslims are safe."[18]

And Bahz bin Ḥakīm reports from his father from his grandfather that he asked the Messenger of Allāh [salallāhu 'alayhi wa sallam] about Islām, so he replied: "To submit your heart to Allāh, turn your face towards Allāh, to perform the obligatory

---

(17) Ṣaḥīḥ Muslim [1/8].

(18) Ṣaḥīḥ al-Bukhārī [10], Ṣaḥīḥ Muslim [64/40].

prayers, and that you pay the obligatory Zakāh."
Narrated by Aḥmad.[19]

And from Abū Qilābah, from a man in the Levant,
from his father, he asked the Messenger of Allāh
[salallāhu 'alayhi wa sallam]: 'What is Islām?' He
replied: "It is to submit your heart to Allāh, and
that the Muslims are safe from your tongue and
your hand." He asked: 'Which Islām is best?' He
said: "Faith." He asked: 'And what is faith?' He said:
"It is to believe in Allāh and His angels, His Books,
His messengers, and resurrection after death."[20]

---

(19) Ḥasan: Musnad Aḥmad [5/3, Ḥadīth 20022, and in
another edition: Ḥadīth 20036] with a Ḥasan Isnād.

(20) Kitāb al-Īmān li Ibn Taymiyyah [p. 158] and Ta'dhīm
qadr aṣ-Ṣalāh lil Marwazī [1/401-402, Ḥadīth 392] and the
Sanad is Ḍa'īf, but it has supporting narrations in Aḥmad
[4/114, Ḥadīth 17027, with a Ḥasan Isnād] and others, so
with them **the narration is Ḥasan.**

Chapter

The statement of Allāh: **"Anyone who seeks a religion other than Islām, never will it be accepted from him."**
[Sūrah Āl-'Imrān 3:85]

Abū Hurayrah, may Allāh be pleased with him, said: the Messenger of Allāh [salallāhu 'alayhi wa sallam] said: "Deeds will come on the Day of Judgment, and prayer will come and say: 'O Rabb, I am the prayer!' He will say: "You are good." Then, charity will come and say: 'O Rabb, I am the charity.' He will say: "You are good." Then, fasting will come, and He will say: 'O Rabb, I am the fasting!' He will say: "You are good." Then, the other deeds will come, and He will say: "You are good." And then Islām will come and say: 'O Rabb, You are Peace, and I am Islām.' And He will say: "You are good. Through you today I will reward and through you I will punish." And Allāh, the Most High, says in His book: **"Anyone who seeks a religion other than Islām, never will it be accepted from him; and in the Hereafter he will be among the losers.""** [Sūrah Āl-'Imrān 3:85] Narrated by Aḥmad.[21]

And it is narrated in aṣ-Ṣaḥīḥ from 'Ā`ishah, may Allāh be pleased with her, that the Messenger of

---

(21) Sanad Ḍa'īf: See Musnad Aḥmad [2/362, Ḥadīth 8742] and Abū 'Abdur-Raḥmān ['Abdullāh bin Aḥmad bin Ḥanbal] said: "'Abbād bin Rāshid is Thiqah, but al-Ḥasan did not hear from Abū Hurayrah.", meaning that he made a mistake in saying from al-Ḥasan: "Abū Hurayrah narrated to me".

And I say: 'Abbād bin Rāshid is Ḍa'īf, he has been declared as such by the majority of scholars.

Allāh [salallāhu 'alayhi wa sallam] said: "Whoever does any action that is not a part of this affair of ours [Islām] will have it rejected." Narrated by Ahmad.[22]

(22) Ṣaḥīḥ, and it has already been mentioned in footnote (10). It was also narrated by Aḥmad [6/146, Ḥadīth 25128, 6/180, Ḥadīth 25472 and 6/256, Ḥadīth 26191].

Chapter
The obligation of sufficing with following, i.e., the Qurān

Allāh, the Most High, says: **"We have sent down to you the Book as an explanation of everything."** [Sūrah an-Naḥl 16:89]

And it is narrated by an-Nasā'ī and others, from Prophet [salallāhu 'alayhi wa sallam], he saw in the hand of 'Umar bin al-Khaṭṭāb, may Allāh be pleased with him, a page from the Tawrāh, upon which he said: "Are you in a state of confusion, O son of Khaṭṭāb? I have come to you with it [the message], radiant and pure. Indeed, if Mūsā were alive and you were to follow him and leave me, you would go astray.", and in another narration: "If Mūsā were alive, he would have no option but to follow me." Thereupon, 'Umar said: 'I am pleased with Allāh as a Rabb, with Islām as a religion, and with Muḥammad as a Prophet.'[23]

---

(23) **Sanad Ḍa'īf**: See Sunan ad-Dārimī [441, and in the edition of Ḥusayn Salīm Asad: 449]. Also see: Musnad Aḥmad [3/387, Ḥadīth 15156] and Mishkāt [with my Taḥqīq: 177]. And I could not find it in an- an-Nasā'ī, and Allāh knows best.

In the chain is Mujālid bin Sa'īd who is weak [as has already been mentioned in footnote **(16)**]. And the supporting narrations are weak as well, see Aḍwā' al-Maṣābīḥ [1/238, Ḥadīth 177].

And there is no doubt in this, that if Mūsā, peace be upon him, was alive, he would have no option other than to follow Muḥammad [salallāhu 'alayhi wa sallam], as is apparent from the Qurān, see Sūrah Āl-'Imrān [3:81].

Chapter
What has been mentioned about attributing oneself to other than Islām

Allāh, the Most High, says: **"He named you as Muslims earlier and in this [Qurān]."** [Sūrah al-Ḥajj 22:78]

Al-Ḥārith al-Ash'arī, may Allāh be pleased with him, narrates from the Messenger of Allāh [salallāhu 'alayhi wa sallam], he said: "I command you with five that Allāh commanded me with: Listening and obeying, Jihād and Hijrah [migration for the sake of Allāh], and adhering to the Jamā'ah [Muslim community]. For indeed, whoever parts from the Muslim community the measure of a hand-span, has cast off the yoke of Islām from his neck, unless he returns. And whoever calls with the call of Jāhiliyyah, is from the coals of Hell." A man said: 'O Messenger of Allāh, even if he prays and fasts?' He said: "Even if he prays and fasts. So, call with the call that Allāh named you with: Muslims, believers, worshippers of Allāh." Narrated by Aḥmad and Tirmidhī who classified it as Ḥasan Ṣaḥīḥ.[24]

And it is transmitted in aṣ-Ṣaḥīḥ: "Whoever abandons the community of Muslims by a hand-span will die a death of Jāhiliyyah."[25]

---

(24) **Ṣaḥīḥ**: Musnad Aḥmad [4/130, Ḥadīth 17170, 4/202, Ḥadīth 17800], Sunan at-Tirmidhī [2863, and he said: 'Ḥasan Ṣaḥīḥ Gharīb'], authenticated by Ibn Ḥibbān [1224, 1550] and al-Ḥākim [1/117-118, 236, 421-422] and adh-Dhahabī agreed with him.

(25) Ṣaḥīḥ al-Bukhārī [7054], Ṣaḥīḥ Muslim [55/1849].

And also: "Is there the call to Jāhiliyyah while I am still among you?!"[26]

Abul-'Abbās[27] said: 'Anything that is foreign to the call of Islām and the Quran – be it lineage, nationality, race, Madhab, or a [Sufi] order [one ascribes to] – is attributed to Jāhiliyyah. When a Muhājir and an Anṣārī were disputing with each other, and the Muhājir said: 'O Muhājirīn!' and the Anṣārī said: 'O Anṣār!', the Messenger of Allāh [salallāhu 'alayhi wa sallam] said: "Is there a call of Jāhiliyyah while I am still among you?!" And he was extremely angry with this.'[28]

---

(26) Ṣaḥīḥ al-Bukhārī [4905], Ṣaḥīḥ Muslim [63/2584].

(27) And he is Shaykhul-Islām Ibn Taymiyyah, may Allāh have mercy on him.

(28) As-Siyāsah ash-Shar'iyyah fī Ādāb ar-Rā'ī war-Ra'iyyah [p. 95].

Chapter

The obligation to enter Islām completely and to abandon everything else

Allāh, the Most High, says: **"O you who believe, enter into Islām completely."** [Sūrah al-Baqarah 2:208]

And He says: **"Have you not seen those who claim that they believe in what has been sent down to you and what was sent down before you."** [Sūrah an-Nisā` 4:60]

And He says: **"Verily, those who divide their religion and break up into sects, you [O Muhammad [salallāhu 'alayhi wa sallam]] have no concern in them in the least."** [Sūrah al-An'ām 6:159]

And He says: **"On the Day [some] faces will turn white and [some] faces will turn black."** [Sūrah Āl-'Imrān 3:106]. Ibn 'Abbās, may Allāh be pleased with him, said: 'The faces of the people of Sunnah and unity will be white, and the faces of the people of religious innovations and disunity will be black.'[29]

'Abdullāh bin 'Amr, may Allah be pleased with them, said, the Messenger of Allāh [salallāhu 'alayhi wa sallam] said: "What befell the Children of Isrā`īl will befall my Ummah, step by step, to such an extent that even if there was someone who had intercourse with his mother in public,

______

(29) **Sanad Ḍa'īf**: Tafsīr Ibn Kathīr [in the print of ash-Shu'b 2/76] and others, and there are issues with the chain of narration to Ibn 'Abbās [for this statement].

then there would be someone from my Ummah who would do the same. Indeed, the Children of Isrāʾīl split into seventy-two sects. And this Ummah will split into seventy-three sects, all of them will be in Hellfire except one." They said: 'Who is it, O Messenger of Allāh?' He said: "[Those who follow] what I and my Companions are upon."[30]

And it is upon a believer who believes in the meeting with Allāh, that he heeds to the words of the Trusted that have been mentioned here, for indeed he is believed. Especially his saying: "What I and my Companions are upon." What a great admonition that sits well with the attentive heart! Tirmidhī narrated it.

And he also narrated it from Abū Hurayrah and declared it Ṣaḥīḥ, but it does not mention the Hellfire.[31]

And it comes in Aḥmad and Abū Dāwūd from the Ḥadīth of Muʿāwiyah: "There will appear among my Ummah some people who will be dominated

---

(30) **Sanad Ḍaʿīf**: Sunan at-Tirmidhī [Book of Īmān, Chapter: What has been transmitted about the splitting that will occur in this Ummah, Ḥadīth 2641, and he said: Ḥasan Ṣaḥīḥ]. **I say**: ʿAbdur-Raḥmān bin Ziyād bin Anʿam al-Ifrīqī is in the chain, and he is known to be weak. And the text of this report has weak supporting narrations.

(31) **Ḥasan**: Sunan at-Tirmidhī [2640, and he said: Ḥasan Ṣaḥīḥ], and the Sanad is Ḥasan li-dhātihi, authenticated by Ibn Ḥibbān [1834] and al-Ḥākim [1/128] on the conditions of Muslim, and adh-Dhahabī agreed with him. [Editor: also see Sunan Ibn Mājah [3992], and the Shaykh said it is authentic.]

by desires just like rabies which penetrates its patient. There remains no vein or joint, but it penetrates it."[32]

And we have already mentioned his statement: "He who innovates something into Islām from the aspects of Jāhiliyyah."[33]

---

(32) **Ḥasan**: Musnad Aḥmad [4/102] and Sunan Abī Dāwūd [4597].

(33) See footnote (12).

Chapter

What has been mentioned regarding innovating [in the religion] is worse than a major sin

Based on the saying of Allāh, the Most High: **"Allāh does not forgive associating partners with Him, but forgives anything less than that for whom He wills."** [Surat an-Nisā` 4:48]

And His saying: **"Then who does more wrong than one who invents a lie against Allāh, to lead mankind astray without knowledge."** [Sūrah al-An'ām 6:144]

And His saying: **"They will bear their burdens in full on the Day of Resurrection and some burdens of those whom they misled without knowledge. How terrible is what they will bear!"** [Surat an-Naḥl 16:25]

And it has been narrated in aṣ-Ṣaḥīḥ that the Prophet [salallāhu 'alayhi wa sallam] said regarding the Khawārij: "Wherever you find them, kill them."(34) ["If I were to meet them, I would kill them like the killing of 'Ād."](35)

It has also been narrated that he forbade the killing of tyrannical rulers so long as they offer the prayer.(36)

It has been narrated from Jarīr bin 'Abdullāh, a man gave charity and then people began to follow suit; thereupon, the Messenger of Allāh [salallāhu

---

(34) Ṣaḥīḥ al-Bukhārī [6930], Ṣaḥīḥ Muslim [154/1066].

(35) Ṣaḥīḥ al-Bukhārī [4351], Ṣaḥīḥ Muslim [1064].

(36) Ṣaḥīḥ Muslim [62-63/1854].

'alayhi wa sallam] said: "Whoever introduces a good practice in Islām, there is for him its reward and the reward of those who act upon it after him without anything being diminished from their rewards. And whoever introduces an evil practice in Islām will shoulder its sin and the sins of all those who will act upon it, without diminishing anything of their burden." Narrated by Muslim.[37] And similar[38] is reported in the Ḥadīth of Abū Hurayrah, and the wording is: "Whosoever calls to guidance" – and then he said – "and whosoever calls to misguidance."

---

(37) Ṣaḥīḥ Muslim [69/1017, 2673].
(38) Ṣaḥīḥ Muslim [16/2674].

Chapter
What has been mentioned regarding Allāh withholding repentance from the person of Bid'ah

This is based on the Hadīth reported by Anas, as part of the Marasīl of al-Ḥasan.[39] And Ibn Waḍḍāḥ mentions from Ayyūb, he said: 'There was a man with us who had adopted ar-Ra`yy [speculative theology] but then abandoned it.' So, I went to Muḥammad bin Sīrīn and said: 'Have you noticed that so-and-so abandoned ar-Ra`yy?' He said: 'Look towards what he has turned to?' For indeed, the latter part of the Hadīth was more severe to them than its beginning: 'They leave Islām like an arrow goes through its target, then they will not return to it.'[40]

---

(39) **Ḥasan:** Al-Bida'u wa-nahī 'anhā [148] from al-Ḥasan al-Baṣrī, and Ḥadīth 149 from Anas bin Mālik, and it has weak supporting narrations in Sunan Ibn Mājah [50] but the Ḥadīth has a supporting narration in al-Awsaṭ by aṭ-Ṭabarānī [4216] with a Ḥasan li-dhātihi Sanad, so the Ḥadīth is Ḥasan.

(40) **Ḥasan:** Al-Bida'u wa-nahı 'anha [147, and in another edition: 155], and the Sanad is Ḥasan li-dhātihi.

Mu`mal bin Ismā'īl is trustworthy, Ḥasanul-Ḥadīth, the majority of Ḥadīth scholars declared him to be Thiqah - trustworthy.

And the Ḥadīth "They leave it...will not return back to it" in Ṣaḥīḥ Muslim [158/1067] has the same meaning.

Aḥmad bin Ḥanbal was asked about the meaning
of this, and he said: 'He is not granted guidance to
repent.'[41]

---

(41) I could not found this statement narrated from him
with a Ṣaḥīḥ Isnād.

Chapter

The statement of Allāh: "O People of the Scripture, why do you argue about Abraham..." Sūrah Āl-'Imrān [3:65]

Allāh, the Most High, says: **"O People of the Scripture, why do you argue about Ibrāhīm? The Torah and Gospel were revealed only after him..."** until His saying: **"...and he was not one of the polytheists."** [Sūrah Āl-'Imrān 3:65-67]

And His saying: **"Who would forsake the religion of Abraham except a fool! We have chosen him in this world, and in the Hereafter, he will be among the righteous."** [Sūrah al-Baqarah 2:130]

The aforementioned Ḥadīth about the Khawārij is also relevant to this chapter, and on this issue, he [salallāhu 'alayhi wa sallam] also said: "The family of the father of so-and-so are not my friends. Indeed, my friends are the pious."[42]

Another Ḥadīth on the subject is narrated by Anas, the Messenger of Allāh [salallāhu 'alayhi wa sallam] was informed that some Companions said: 'As for me, I will not eat meat.' And another said: 'As for me, then I will stand up in prayer and will not sleep.' And another one said: 'As for me, then I will not marry any woman.' And another one said: 'And as for me, I will observe fast and not break it.' So, he [salallāhu 'alayhi wa sallam] said: "But I stand [in prayer] and I also sleep, I fast and also break my fast, and I marry women, and I eat meat.

---

(42) Ṣaḥīḥ al-Bukhārī [5990], Ṣaḥīḥ Muslim [215].

So, whoever abandons my Sunnah does not belong to me."[43]

This observation should be carefully considered! If some of the Companions wanted to be entirely devoted to worship and, as a result, they heard such harsh rebuke and their acts were regarded as a renouncement of the Sunnah, Then how severe is the matter for those who indulge/practice [religious] innovations and who do not even rank among the Companions?!

---

[43] Ṣaḥīḥ al-Bukhārī [5063], Ṣaḥīḥ Muslim [5/1401]. [Editor: The references do not mention the part: "and I eat meat", although of course the Prophet [salallāhu 'alayhi wa sallam] would eat meat, see Ṣaḥīḥ al-Bukhārī [5400, 5405, 5408] and many other such narrations].

Chapter
The statement of Allāh: "Adhere sincerely to the true religion in all uprightness..."
Sūrah ar-Rūm [30:30]

Allāh, the Most High, says: **"Adhere sincerely to the true religion in all uprightness. This is the natural disposition with which Allāh has created mankind. There is no change in Allāh's creation. This is the straight religion, but most people do not know."** [Sūrah ar-Rūm 30:30]

And He says: **"This was enjoined by Ibrāhīm and Ya'qūb to their offspring, 'O my children, Allāh has chosen for you this religion; so, do not die except as Muslims.'"** [Sūrah al-Baqarah 2:132]

And He says: **"Then We revealed to you [O Prophet] to follow the religion of Abraham, inclining to true faith, and he was not one of those who associate partners with Allāh."** [Sūrah an-Naḥl 16:123]

Ibn Mas'ūd, may Allāh be pleased with him narrates, the Messenger of Allāh [salallāhu 'alayhi wa sallam] said: "Every prophet has allies among the prophets, and my ally among them is my father Ibrāhīm [Abraham] who is also the friend of my Rabb." Then he recited: **"The closest people to Ibrāhīm are those who followed him, and this Prophet and those who believe. And Allāh is the Guardian of the believers."** [Sūrah Āl-'Imrān 3:68]. Narrated by Tirmidhī.[44]

---

(44) Sanad Ḍa'īf: See Sunan at-Tirmidhī [2995]. Sufyān ath-Thawrī is in the chain who is a Mudallis, and he narrated

Abū Hurayrah, may Allāh be pleased with him narrated, the Messenger of Allāh [salallāhu 'alayhi wa sallam] said: "Allāh does not look at your bodies or your wealth, but He looks at your hearts and deeds."(45)

And it is narrated in both [Ṣaḥīḥ collections, i.e., Bukhārī and Muslim] from Ibn Mas'ūd, may Allāh be pleased with him, the Messenger of Allāh [salallāhu 'alayhi wa sallam] said: "I am your predecessor at the Ḥawḍ [Cistern] and I will recognize some men amongst my Ummah, and when I try to hand them some water, they will be pulled away from me by force; so I will say: "O Rabb, my companions!" Then, it will be said: 'You do not know what they innovated after you.'(46)

And it is narrated in both from Abū Hurayrah, may Allāh be pleased with him, the Messenger of Allāh [salallāhu 'alayhi wa sallam] said: "I wish to see my brothers." They said: 'Are we not your brothers, O Messenger of Allāh?' He said: "You are my Companions, and our brothers are those that come afterwards." They said: 'O Messenger of Allāh, how will you recognize the people of your Ummah who are not yet born?' He said: "Suppose a man had horses with white blazes on the

---

with "عن", and al-Ḥākim still authenticated it on the conditions of Bukhārī and Muslim [2/292] and adh-Dhahabī agreed with him!

(45) Ṣaḥīḥ Muslim [34/2564] with a similar meaning.

(46) Ṣaḥīḥ al-Bukhārī [6576], Ṣaḥīḥ Muslim [32/2297]. [Editor: Part of the wording is from Ṣaḥīḥ al-Bukhārī [7049].]

foreheads and legs among horses which were all black; tell me, would he not recognize his own horses?" They said: 'Certainly!' He said: "They will come with white faces and arms and legs owing to ablution, and I will arrive at the Cistern before them. Some people will be driven away from my Cistern on the Day of Judgement as the stray camel is driven away. I will call out: 'Come, come.' So, it will be said: 'These people changed after you.' So, I will say: "Be off, be off. "(47)

And in al-Bukhārī: "While I was sleeping, a group [of my followers were brought close to me], and when I recognized them, a man [an angel] came out from between me and them and said [to them]: 'Come along.' I asked: "Where?" He said: 'To Hellfire, by Allāh!' I asked: "What is wrong with them?" He said: "They turned apostates and renegades after you left." Then, behold! Another group was brought close to me [and he related the same occurrence and said:] So, I did not see anyone of them escaping, except a few who were [rare] like camels without a shepherd."(48)

And it is narrated in both from Ibn 'Abbās, may Allāh be pleased with him and his father, that he [[salallāhu 'alayhi wa sallam]] said: 'Thereupon, I will say as the righteous servant said: **"I was a witness over them as long as I was among them. But when You took me up, You Yourself were**

---

(47) Ṣaḥīḥ Muslim [39/249] with this wording.
(48) Ṣaḥīḥ al-Bukhārī [6587].

Watcher over them, and You are a Witness over all things." [Sūrah al-Mā`idah 5:117][49]

And both narrated from the Prophet [salallāhu 'alayhi wa sallam]: "There is no child, but he is born upon the Fiṭrah [natural disposition]. It is his parents who make him a Jew, a Christian or a Magian. Like the beasts that give birth to their young with perfect limbs – do you see anything deficient in them unless you make them deficient?" Then, Abū Hurayrah, may Allāh be pleased with him, recited: **"This is the natural disposition with which Allāh has created mankind."** [Sūrah ar-Rūm 30:30] Muttafaqun 'alayh.[50]

And it is narrated from Ḥudhayfah, may Allāh be pleased with him, he said: "The people used to ask the Messenger of Allāh [salallāhu 'alayhi wa sallam] about the good, but I used to ask him about the evil for fear that it might overtake me. Once I said: 'O Messenger of Allāh, we were in ignorance and in evil and Allāh bestowed upon us the present good; will there be any evil after this good?' He said: "Yes." I asked: 'Will there be good after that evil?' He said: "Yes, but it will be tainted." I asked: 'What will it be tainted with?' He said: "There will be some people who will lead [people] according to other than my Sunnah. And they will [try to] guide people with other than my guidance [that I came with]. You will recognize them and disapprove of them." I said: 'Will there be any evil

---

(49) Ṣaḥīḥ al-Bukhārī [4625], Ṣaḥīḥ Muslim [58/2860].

(50) Ṣaḥīḥ al-Bukhārī [1358], Ṣaḥīḥ Muslim [22/2658].

after that good?' He said: "Yes, trials that will blind the people[51], and there will be some people who will invite others to the doors of Hell, and whoever accepts their invitation to it will be thrown in it." I said: 'O Messenger of Allāh, describe those people to us.'

He said: "They will belong to us and speak our language." I asked: 'O Messenger of Allāh! What do you order me to do if such a thing should take place in my life?' He said: "Adhere to the community of Muslims and their ruler." I asked: 'And if there is neither a community nor a ruler?' He said: "Keep away from all the different sects, even if you have to bite onto the root of a tree, till death comes to you while you are still in that state." Both al-Bukhārī and Muslim narrated it. [52]

And Muslim has the addition: 'What will come next?' He replied: "Then the Dajjāl will come forth accompanied by a river and a fire. He who falls into his fire will certainly receive his reward and his load will be taken off him." I then asked: 'What will come next?' He said: "The Last Hour will come."[53]

Abul-'Āliyah said: 'Learn Islām, and when you learn it, do not abandon it. And upon you is [following] the straight path, for this is Islām, and

---

(51) [Editor: Also refer to Shaykh Zubayr 'Alī Za'i's checking of the Sunan Abū Dawūd [4246]. He says: "The chain is authentic – and it was transmitted by Ahmad [5/386], Nasā'ī in al-Kubra [8032].

(52) Ṣaḥīḥ Bukhārī [4625], Ṣaḥīḥ Muslim [58/2860].

(53) Ṣaḥīḥ Muslim [2934-2935] with a slight variation.

do not swerve from the path to the right or the left. And upon you is the Sunnah of your Prophet and beware of these [deviant] desires.'[54] End quote.

Consider these insightful words by Abul-'Āliyah[55], learn about the era in which he warned of such deviant desires that may lead one to be averse to Islām, reflect on how he explains Islām with the Sunnah, and his fear for the flag-bearers and the scholars amongst the Tābi'īn that they might abandon the Qurān and Sunnah. This will make clear to you the meaning of the statement of the Most High: **"When his Rabb said to him, "Submit!". He said: "I have submitted myself to the Rabb of the worlds.""** [Sūrah al-Baqarah 2:131] And His saying: **"This was enjoined by Ibrāhīm and Ya'qūb**

(**54**) Ṣaḥīḥ: As-Sunnah lil Marwazī [18] with a Ṣaḥīḥ Isnād, and ash-Sharī'ah lil Ājurrī [Ḥadīth 19] [Editor: The report continues and mentions, 'Āṣim Aḥwāl said: I informed al-Ḥasan [al-Baṣrī] what Abul-'Āliyyah had said. He replied: "He spoke the truth and advise you with it." Then I narrated this to Hafṣah bint Sirīn and she said: "You are family, have you narrated this to Muḥammad?" I said: "No". She said: "Narrate this to him." [Imām Muḥammad bin Naṣr al-Marwazī, as-Sunnah [narration 18, page 68-69 the print by Dār al-Athār, 2003, Cairo].

(**55**) [Editor: He was an early scholar, he was a young boy and alive during the time of Allāh's Messenger [salallāhu 'alayhi wa sallam] but accepted Islām during the time of Abū Bakr, may Allāh be pleased with him. He heard Ḥadīth from senior Companions, and is recognised as a senior Tābi'ī. He died in Basrah in 93AH, see Tabaqāt Ibn Sa'd [7/112], Tarīkh al-Kabīr of al-Bukhārī [3/326], Tahdhīb al-Kamāl [9/215], Tahdhīb ut-Tahdhīb [3/284], Siyar A'lām an-Nubalā [4/207, number 85], Tadhkirratul Ḥuffāẓ [1/58], Tārīkh al-Islām [3/19] and many others].

to their offspring, "O my children, Allāh has chosen for you this religion; so, do not die except as Muslims."" [Sūrah al- Baqarah 2:132] And His saying: "Who would forsake the religion of Ibrāhīm except a fool!" [Sūrah al-Baqarah 2:130] You will then be able to clearly understand principles similar to the ones mentioned above, which are the fundamental principles of all principles that people are heedless of. And by recognizing this, the meaning of the Aḥādīth in this chapter and similar ones will become clear to you. A person who reads those and other similar Aḥādīth, and he feels safe in that they do not apply to him and thinking that they only address other people, then destruction [is feared for him]: "Did they then feel secure against the Plan of Allāh. None feels secure from the Plan of Allāh except the people who are the losers." [Sūrah al-A'rāf 7:99]

And Ibn Mas'ūd, may Allāh be pleased with him, reported: The Messenger of Allāh [salallāhu 'alayhi wa sallam] drew a line for us and said: "This is the path of Allāh." Then he drew several lines on his right and left and said: "These are paths on each of which there is a devil who invites to it." And he recited: "This is My straight path; follow it and do not follow other ways, lest they lead you away from His way." [Sūrah al-An'ām 6:153]. Narrated by Aḥmad and an-Nasā`ī.[56]

---

(56) Ḥasan: Musnad Aḥmad [1/435, Ḥadīth 4142 with a Ḥasan Isnād, 1/465, Ḥadīth 4437], an-Nasā`ī in al-Kubrā [11174] and it is a Ḥasan Ḥadīth, authenticated by Ibn Ḥibbān [6-7] and al-Ḥākim [2/318] and adh-Dhahabī agreed with him.

Chapter
What has been mentioned regarding the strangeness of Islām and the merits of the strangers

And Allāh, the Most High, says: **"If only there had been among the generations before you righteous people who would forbid others from spreading corruption in the land, except a few of them whom We saved."** [Surat Hūd 11:116].

And Abū Hurayrah, may Allāh be pleased with him, reports from the Prophet [salallāhu 'alayhi wa sallam]: "Islām began as something strange and will return to being strange; so glad tidings to the strangers." Narrated by Muslim.[57]

And Aḥmad narrates this Ḥadīth from Ibn Mas'ūd, which mentions: 'Who are the strangers?' He said: "Those who left their family and tribes."[58] And in another narration: "The strangers are those that remain steadfast upon good when people become corrupt."[59]

And in Sunan at-Tirmidhī from the Ḥadīth reported by Kathīr bin 'Abdullāh from his father

---

(57) Ṣaḥīḥ Muslim [232/145].

(58) **Sanad Ḍa'īf**: See Musnad Aḥmad [1/398, Ḥadīth 3784] [and Sunan Ibn Mājah, Ḥadīth 3988]. Ḥafṣ bin Ghiyāth, Sulaymān al-A'mash and Abū Isḥāq are Mudallisīn and they narrate with "عن".

(59) **Ḥasan**: Musnad Aḥmad [1/184, Ḥadīth 1604], al-Īmān li Ibn Mandah [424], and the name of Ibn Las'ad is 'Āmir, and he is known to be Thiqah.

from his grandfather: "Glad tidings to the strangers – those who correct what the people have corrupted from my Sunnah after me."[60]

And Abū Umayyah related: I asked Abū Tha'labah: 'O Abū Tha'labah! What do you say about [the meaning of] the Āyah: **"O you who believe, take care of your own selves. Those who have gone astray will not harm you as long as you are guided."'** [Sūrah al-Mā`idah 5:105]

He said: 'Indeed, by Allāh, I asked a well-informed one about it. I asked the Messenger of Allāh [salallāhu 'alayhi wa sallam] about it, and he said: "Rather, command what is good and forbid what is evil, until you see greed obeyed, desires followed, and the worldly life preferred, and everyone is amazed with his own view. Then you should be concerned about yourself and have no concern about the common folk. Ahead of you are the days in which patience is like holding onto hot coal, for the one who does [righteous deeds] during them has the reward of fifty of those who do the like of what you do." It was said: 'The reward [of fifty men] among us, or them?' He said: "Rather, [the reward of fifty men] among you!"' Narrated by Abū Dāwūd and at-Tirmidhī.[61]

Ibn Waḍḍāḥ related a similar Ḥadīth from Ibn 'Umar, may Allāh be pleased with him. And the

---

(60) **Sanad Ḍa'īf Jiddan**: Kathīr bin 'Abdullāh al-'Awfī is Matrūk [rejected]. Sunan at-Tirmidhī [2630, and he said: Ḥasan].

(61) **Ḥasan**: Sunan Abū Dāwūd [4341], Sunan at-Tirmidhī [3058, and he said: Ḥasan Gharīb], and the Sanad is Ḥasan.

wording is: "After your era, there will be days in which a person patiently holds onto his religion as you do today and they will have the reward of fifty from among you." It was said: 'O Messenger of Allāh! From among them?' He said: "Rather, [fifty] from you."[62]

Then he said: Muḥammad bin Sa'īd related from Asad that Sufyān bin 'Uyaynah said: from Aslam al-Baṣrī from Sa'īd, Ḥasan's brother and he attributed it to the Prophet [salallāhu 'alayhi wa sallam]. I said to Sufyān: 'He attributed it the Prophet [salallāhu 'alayhi wa sallam]?' He said: 'Yes.' It said: "Today, you are upon clarity from your Rabb. You command the good, forbid the evil, and engage in Jihād in the cause of Allāh. So far, the two consider changing to pains or anguishes have not emerged among you: the anguish of ignorance and the anguish of loving to live long. Things will later change with no commanding the good and forbidding the evil, and no Jihād in the cause of Allāh, and the two anguishes will become apparent amongst you. Then anyone holding fast onto the Qurān and the Sunnah will be granted the

---

(62) **Sanad Ḍa'īf**: Al-Bida'u wa-nahī 'anhā [188, in another edition: 205] and it has 'Adī bin al-Faḍl in the chain: There are two of them [with the same name] One of them is Thiqah and the second one is Matrūkul-Ḥadīth. And Ibn 'Ijlān is a Mudallis and he narrates with "عن" [so it is still weak even] if the chain was authentic to him. And the previous narration is sufficient.

reward of fifty." It was said: 'From among them?' He said: "Rather, from among you."[63]

And another chain on the authority of al-Mu'āfirī who said: The Messenger of Allāh [salallāhu 'alayhi wa sallam] said: "Glad tidings to the strangers, who hold onto the Qurān when it is abandoned and act on the Sunnah when it vanishes."[64]

---

(63) **Sanad Ḍa'īf**: Al-Bida'u wa-nahī 'anhā [189, in another edition: 206]. And Abū Nu'aym in Ḥilyatul Awliyā` [8/49] from the Ḥadīth of Sa'īd bin Abī al-Ḥusayn from Anas bin Mālik, may Allāh be pleased with him. The integrity or condition of Aslam al-Baṣrī is unknown – Mahjūl al-Ḥāl.

(64) **Sanad Ḍa'īf**: Al-Bida'u wa-nahī 'anhā [169, in another edition: 185] and Mu'āfirī is: Bakr bin 'Amr, and the Sanad - chain of narration is Mursal [disconnected and stops at a Tābi'ī].

Chapter
Warning against innovating [in the religion]

Al-'Irbāḍ bin Sāriyah reported: "The Messenger of Allāh [salallāhu 'alayhi wa sallam] gave us an eloquent admonition which caused the eyes to shed tears and the hearts to become afraid. We said: 'O Messenger of Allāh! It is as if this were a farewell sermon, so advise us.' He said: "I advise you to fear Allāh and to hear and obey, even if a slave is put in charge of you. Any of you who live after me will witness much differing. So, upon you is to hold fast to my Sunnah and the Sunnah of the rightly guided Caliphs after me. Bite onto it with your molar teeth. And beware of innovated matters, for indeed every [religious] innovation is misguidance." Tirmidhī said: The Ḥadīth is Ḥasan Ṣaḥīḥ.[65]

And from Ḥudhayfah: 'Any act of worship that was not performed by the Companions of Muḥammad, do not perform it. The former generation have not left anything to be decided by the latter generations. So, fear Allāh, O community of Reciters, and follow the path of those who came before you.' Narrated by Abū Dāwūd.[66]

---

(65) **Ṣaḥīḥ**: Sunan at-Tirmidhī [2676] who said Ḥasan-Ṣaḥīḥ, Sunan Abū Dawūd [607], Ibn Ḥibban authenticated it [102], as well as al-Ḥākim [1/95-96], adh-Dhahabī and others.

(66) I could not find an authentic chain to him. I could not find this in Abū Dawūd's Sunan or his az-Zuhd, in fact I was not able to find a continuous chain for this narration to him at all, and Allāh knows best.

And Ad-Dārimī narrated: Al-Ḥakam bin Mubārak related to us that 'Amr [and] Ibn Yaḥyā said: I heard my father relating from his father, saying: 'We used to sit at the door of 'Abdullāh bin Mas'ūd before the Fajr prayer. When he went out, we would walk with him to the Masjid. Once Abū Mūsā al-Ash'arī came and asked: 'Has Abū 'Abdur-Raḥmān[67] come out?' We said: 'No.' So, he sat with us, and when he came out, we all stood up. Abū Mūsā said to him: 'O Abū 'Abdur-Raḥmān, I saw something in the Masjid which I deemed to be evil, but all praise is for Allāh, I did not see anything except good.' He said: 'Then what is it?' He said: "If you live, you will see it. I saw in the Masjid people sitting in circles awaiting the prayer. In each circle there was a man, and in their hands, they had pebbles, and the man would say: 'Say Allāhu Akbar a hundred times.' So, they would say the Takbīr a hundred times. Then he would say: 'Say Lā ilāha ilAllāh a hundred times.' So, they would say the Tahlīl a hundred times. Then he would say: 'Say SubḥānAllāh a hundred times.' So, they would say Tasbīḥ a hundred times.' He [Ibn Mas'ūd] asked: 'And what did you say to them?' He [Abū Mūsā] said: 'I did not say anything to them. Instead, I was waiting to hear your view and what you order.' He replied: 'Would that you had ordered them to count up their evil deeds, and assured them that their good deeds would not be lost.' Then we went along with him until he reached one of these circles and stopped, and said:

---

(67) [Editor: Abū 'Abdur-Raḥmān is the Kunyā (nickname) of 'Abdullāh bin Mas'ūd, may Allāh be pleased with him].

'What is this which I see you doing?' They replied: 'O Abū 'Abdur-Raḥmān! These are pebbles upon which we are counting Takbīr, Tahlīl and Taṣbīḥ.' He said: 'Count up your evil deeds. I assure you that none of your good deeds will be lost. Woe to you, O Ummah of Muḥammad! How quickly you go to destruction! These are the Companions of your Prophet [salallāhu 'alayhi wa sallam] and they are widespread. And here are his clothes which have not yet decayed and his bowl which has not yet broken. By Him in Whose Hand is my soul! Either you are upon a Religion better guided than the Religion of Muḥammad or you are opening the door of misguidance!' They said: 'O Abū 'Abdur-Raḥmān! By Allāh, we only intended good!' He said: 'And how many there are who intend good but do not achieve it. Indeed, the Messenger of Allāh [salallāhu 'alayhi wa sallam] said to us: "A people will recite the Qur'ān but it will not pass beyond their throats." By Allāh! I do not know, perhaps most of them are from you.' Then he left them. And 'Umar bin Salamah said: 'We saw most of the people of those circles fighting against us on the day of Nahrawān, along with the Khawārij." [68]

And this is the end of what was made easy for me. [Mu'allafāt ash-Shaykh al-Imām Muḥammad bin 'Abdul-Wahhāb, 1/205-227].

[End of Taḥqīq of Ḥāfiẓ Zubayr 'Alī Za'ī, Makkah al-Mukarramah, 1st September 2003, and the revision was completed on the 20th May 2013 in Maktabah al-Ḥadīth Ḥaḍro, Attock]

---

(68) **Ḥasan**: Sunan ad-Dārimī [210].

A Summarised Biography
of the Muḥaqqiq

Name and lineage: Abū Mu'ādh Muḥammad Zubayr bin Mujaddid Khān bin Dost Muḥammad Khān bin Jahāngīr 'Alī-Za`ī al-Afghānī al-Pākistānī

Birth: 1376AH (i.e., the year 1957)

Shuyūkh: He took Ijāzāt from many Shuyūkh. From them:

1. Shaykh Abū Muḥammad Badī' ud-Dīn Shāh ar-Rāshdī as-Sindhī,

2. Shaykh Abul-Qāsim Muḥibullāh Shāh ar-Rāshdī as-Sindhī,

3. Shaykh Abul-Faḍl Fayḍur-Raḥmān Thawrī, the author of ar-Radd at-Taqī 'alal-Jawhar an-Naqī,

4. Shaykh Abur-Rijāl Allāh-ditta as-Suhdarwī al-Ahwarī,

5. Shaykh 'Abdul-Ghaffār Ḥasan ar-Raḥmānī,

6. Shaykh 'Aṭā`ullāh Ḥanīf al-Bhojiyan Awjiyānī, the author of at-Ta'liqāt as-Salafiyyah,

7. Shaykh al-Ḥāfiẓ 'Abdul-Mannān Nūrpūrī, the author of Irshādul Qārī,

and other than them, may Allāh have mercy upon all of them.

He graduated from the Jāmi'ah Muḥammadiyyah (Gujranwala) and it is a well-known Jami'ah of the Ahlul-Ḥadīth in Pākistān.

Similarly, he received his certificate for the 'Ālamiyyah course with the grade "Excellent" from the Wifāqul-Madāris as-Salafiyyah (Pākistān).

His books and knowledge-based writings:

He has a lot of books in Urdu and Arabic (see Nūrul-'Aynayn, pp.14-17).

These are the names of his Arabic books:

1. Aḍwā` al-Maṣābīḥ fī Taḥqīq Mishkāt Al-Maṣābīḥ (Manuscript)[69]

2. Al-Asanīd aṣ-Ṣaḥīḥah fī Akhbār al-Imām Abī Ḥanīfah (Manuscript)

3. Anwār as-Sabīl fī Mīzān al-Jarḥ wa Ta'dīl (Manuscript)

---

(69) [Editor: The Taḥqīq with its Urdu translation has been published by Maktaba Islāmiyah, Lahore, Pakistan].

4. Anwār as-Sunan fī Takhrīj wa Taḥqīq Athār as-Sunan (Manuscript)[70]

5. Anwār aṣ-Ṣaḥīfah fil-Aḥādīth aḍ-Ḍa'īfah (Published)

6. Tuḥfatul-Aqwiyā` fī Taḥqīq Kitāb aḍ-Ḍu'afā` (Published)

7. Taḥqīq wa Takhrīj Tafsīr Ibn Kathīr (Published)

8. Taḥqīq Masā`il Muḥammad bin 'Uthmān bin Abī Shaybah [Editor: Published]

9. Taḥqīq wa Takhrīj Aḥādīth Ithbāt 'Adhāb al-Qabr lil Bayhaqī (Manuscript)

10. Taḥqīq wa Takhrīj Bulūgh al-Marām [Editor: Not printed anymore]

11. Taḥqīq wa Takhrīj Juz` 'Alī bin Muḥammad al-Ḥumayrī (Published)

12. Taḥqīq wa Takhrīj Sunan at-Tirmidhī (Published)

13. Taḥqīq wa Takhrīj Kitāb al-Arba'īn li Ibn Taymiyyah (Manuscript)[71]

14. Taḥqīq wa Takhrīj Musnad al-Ḥumaydī (Manuscript)

---

(70) [Editor: This has been published by Maktaba Islāmiyyah].

(71) [Editor: This has been published with its summarised Urdu translation by Maktabah Islāmiyah. Salafi Research Institute (UK) recently published its English translation, walḥamdulilāh].

15. Taḥqīq wa Takhrīj Manāqib 'Alī wal-Ḥasnayn wa Ummahumā Fāṭimatuz-Zahrā` (Manuscript)

16. Taḥqīq wa Takhrīj Muwaṭṭā Imām Mālik, Riwāyatu Yaḥyā bin Yaḥyā (Manuscript)

17. Takhrīj al-Anwār fī Shamā`il an-Nabī al-Mukhtār (Manuscript)

18. Takhrīj an-Nihāyah fil-Fitan wal-Malāḥim (Muṭawwal, Manuscript)

19. Takhrīj Aḥadīth Minhāj al-Muslim (Manuscript)

20. Takhrīj Juz` Raf'ul-Yadayn lil Bukhārī (Manuscript)[72]

21. Takhrīj Shi'ār Aṣḥābul-Ḥadīth li Abī Aḥmad al-Ḥākim (Manuscript)

22. Takhrīj Kitāb al-Jihād li Ibn Taymiyyah (Manuscript)

23. Takhrīj an-Nihāyah fil-Fitn wal-Malāḥim (Mukhtaṣar, Manuscript)

24. Takhrīj wa Taḥqīq al-Mu'jam aṣ-Ṣaghīr li Ṭabarānī (Incomplete)

25. Tashīl al-Ḥājah fī Taḥqīq wa Takhrīj Sunan Ibn Mājah (Manuscript)

---

[72] [Editor: This has been published with its Urdu translation by Maktabah Islāmiyah].

26. Al-Taqbīl wal-Mu'ānaqah li Ibn al-'Arabī, Taḥqīq wa Takhrīj (Manuscript)[73]

27. Talkhīṣ al-Kāmil li Ibn 'Adī

28. As-Sirāj al-Munīr fī Takhrīj Tafsīr Ibn Kathīr (Lost)

29. Ṣaḥīḥ at-Tafasīr (Incomplete, Manuscript)

30. Al-'Aqd at-Tamām fī Taḥqīq Sīrah li Ibn Hishām (Manuscript)

31. 'Umdatul-Masā'ī fī Taḥqīq wa Takhrīj Sunan an-Nasā`ī (Manuscript)

32. Al-Fatḥ al-Mubīn fī Taḥqīq Ṭabaqāt al-Mudallisīn (Published)

33. Faḍl al-Islām lī ash-Shaykh Muḥammad bin 'Abdul-Wahhāb (Published)

34. Fī ẓilāl as-Sunnah (Published in Siyāḥatul-Ummah, Islāmabād)

35. Kalām ad-Daraquṭnī fī naqd ar-Rijāl, fī Sunanihi (Manuscript)

36. Nayl al-Maqṣūd fī Taḥqīq wa Takhrīj Sunan Abī Dawūd (Manuscript)

37. Taḥqīq wa Takhrīj Ḥisnul Muslim (Published)

38. Taḥqīq wa Takhrīj Ṣaḥīḥ Ibn Khuzaimah[74]

---

(73) [Editor: This has been published with its Urdu translation by Maktabah Islāmiyah].

(74) [Editor: The son of Ḥāfiẓ Zubayr 'Alī Za'ī [raḥimahullāh], Ḥāfiẓ Mu'ādh, is currently working on a

39. Al-Itḥāf al-Bāsim (Taḥqīq wa Takhrīj Muwaṭṭa Rawāyatu Ibn al-Qāsim)[75]

and other books.

And he is the director of the monthly magazine "Ishā'atul-Ḥadīth", published in Ḥaḍro in the Urdu language, and more than 100 issues have been published already.[76]

[Editor: Ḥāfiẓ Zubayr ʿAlī Zaʾī [raḥimahullāh] passed away on the 10th November 2013 at the age of 56.]

Takhrīj and Urdu translation of Ṣaḥīḥ Ibn Khuzaimah, may Allāh grant him success, Ameen].

(75) [Editor: This has been published with its Urdu translation by Maktaba Islāmiyyah].

(76) [Editor: In March 2021 the last edition of the magazine was published. All 147 editions are freely available on ishaatulhadith.com and on the "IshaatulHadith"-App, which contains many of the books of Ḥāfiẓ Zubayr ʿAlī Zaʾī [raḥimahullāh] any they can be accessed free of charge.

Praise of
Shaykh Dr. Waṣiullāh Abbās for Ḥāfiẓ Zubayr ‘Alī Za’ī(77)

الحمد للہ ربّ العالمین والصّلٰوۃ والسّلام علیٰ خیر خلقہ محمد وعلیٰ آلہ وصحبہ أجمعین، وبعد:

مولانا حافظ زبیر علی زئی رحمہ اللہ کی وفات کی خبر سے دل بہت متاثر ہوا، افسوس کی حد نہ رہی، کیونکہ مولانا ایک مخلص اہل حدیث عالم، نیز بڑے پائے کے محقق تھے، حدیث اور علم حدیث میں اچھا درک اور عالی مقام رکھتے تھے ...... علامۂ زماں محدث کبیر شیخنا بدیع الدین الراشدی، علامۂ وقت شیخ الحدیث محمد گوندلوی اور مولانا عبد الغفار حسن رحمہم اللہ جیسے اساطین حدیث وسنت کے فیض یافتہ تھے۔ دین خالص یعنی مسلک سلف کے دفاع، مختلف فیہ مسائل، نیز اختلافی اجتماعی مسائل سے متعلق آپ کی تالیفات دین خالص کے تبعین کے لیے بڑا ذخیرہ ہیں، نیز آپ کے بعد آپ کی یہ تالیفات صدقہ جاریہ ہوں گی، ان شاءاللہ۔

اردو اور عربی زبان میں آپ کی علمی تالیفات اہل علم کے یہاں مقبول ہیں اور آپ کے لیے دعاؤں کا ذریعہ ہیں۔ آپ سے میرا تعارف غائبانہ طور پر بذریعہ فون ہوا تھا، کچھ علم حدیث کے مسائل آپ سے متعلق بات ہوئی تھی، پھر جب مکہ مکرمہ میں آپ کی آمد ہوئی تو گھر پر تشریف لائے اور ہماری خصوصی مجلسیں بھی رہیں۔ ہمارے درمیان حدیث سے متعلق تبادلۂ خیال بھی ہوتا رہا۔ تصحیح حدیث میں آپ متشدد علماء کی رائے پر رہے۔

ہر زمانے میں آپ جیسے محققین کی ضرورت رہی ہے، خصوصاً اس زمانے میں جب کہ بعض اسلامی فرقے دین خالص کے چہرے کو بدگار کرنے کی کوششیں کر رہے ہیں۔ آپ جیسی باہمت قد آور شخصیت کی بڑی ضرورت تھی، لیکن اللہ رب العزت حکیم وخبیر مصلحتوں کو جانتا ہے۔

مولانا نے مجھے بتایا تھا کہ آپ کے معزز والد نے آپ کو علم اور تعلیم وتعلم کے لیے متفرغ کر رکھا تھا، اس وجہ سے آپ نے اپنے اوقات کو مطالعہ وتالیف ہی میں گذارا، آپ نے حدیث وعلم حدیث وفقہ مذاہب سے متعلق بڑا قیمتی مکتبہ بھی جمع کیا ہے، اللہ رب العزت مکتبہ کو حوادث الزمان سے محفوظ رکھ کر اس سے استفادے کو جاری رکھنے کے اسباب مہیا فرمائے۔ (آمین)

دعا ہے کہ اللہ تعالیٰ آپ کی اولاد کو بھی اس لائق بنائے کہ دین خالص پر چل کر والد محترم کی طرح دین کی خدمت کریں اور مکتبہ سے استفادہ کریں۔ آمین

---

(77) This appendix has been added by the editor.

When he heard of the death of Ḥāfiẓ Zubayr ʿAlī Zaʾī [raḥimahullāh], the Mufti of Medīnah and Professor at Umm al-Qura University (Makkah), Shaykh Dr. Waṣiullāh Abbās [ḥafiẓahullāh], wrote the following letter:

"All praise belong to Allāh, the Rabb of the Worlds, and Ṣalāt and Salām be upon the best of creation, Muḥammad, and his family and all his companions. To proceed:

When I heard of the passing away of Maulāna Ḥāfiz Zubayr ʿAlī Zaʿī [raḥimahullāh], my heart felt great pain. The sorrow knows no bounds, as the Maulāna was an honest [Mukhlis] ʾĀlim of the Ahlul-Ḥadīth in addition to being a great Muḥaqqiq.

He had a high station in the field of Ḥadīth and its sciences, and he was very attentive to it. He benefitted with regards to Ḥadīth and the Sunnah from teachers like the ʾAllāma of this time-period, the great Muḥaddith, my Shaykh, Badīʿ ud-Dīn ar-Rāshidi, the ʾAllāma of this time, Shaykhul-Ḥadīth Muḥammad Ghondalwī and Maulāna ʾAbdul-Ghaffār Ḥasan [raḥimahumullāh].

His works in defending the Pure Religion, i.e. the Maslak [methodology] of the Salaf, his works on differed upon matters, as well as differences and agreed upon matters, are a vast treasure for those who follow the Pure Religion, and in shā Allāh these works will continue to be a Ṣadaqah Jāria [ongoing charity] after his passing away. His knowledge based writings in Urdu and Arabic are accepted [Maqbūl] among the People of Knowledge and a source of them supplicating for him [...]

With regards to authenticating Aḥadīth, he followed to way of the Mutashaddid [stern] 'Ulamā. Every era has needed Muḥaqqiqs like him, especially this era, where some Islāmic sects are trying to malign the face of the Pure Religion. There was a great need for such courageous individuals such as him, but Allāh, the Rabb of Honor, the All-Wise and All-Aware knows what is better [...]

He also collected a valuable Maktabah [library] regarding the books of Ḥadīth and the various Fiqhī Madhāhib. May Allāh preserve this Maktabah from any harm so that people may continue to benefit from it, Amīn. I pray to Allāh that He gives his progeny the ability to serve the religion as their revered father did, while they remain faithful to the Pure Religion, and that they benefit from the Maktabah, Amīn."[78]

[End quote]

---

(78) Al-Ḥadīth, Muḥaddithul 'Asr Edition [p. 295].

Visit: **takhrijalhadith-bookstore.net**

Contact **sales@takhrijalhadith.com**
for wholesale orders.

Follow us on **Social Media**:

Linktree: https://linktr.ee/takhrijalhadith